Cooking
SCHOOL

Chinese Food

SARA GILBERT

CREATIVE EDUCATION & CREATIVE PAPERBACKS

Published by Creative Education and Creative Paperbacks
P.O. Box 227, Mankato, Minnesota 56002 • Creative Education
and Creative Paperbacks are imprints of The Creative Company
www.thecreativecompany.us

Design and production by Christine Vanderbeek
Printed in the United States of America

Photographs by Corbis (Liu Liqun), Dreamstime (Frank Hermers),
iStockphoto (naelnabil, Naphat_Jorjee, Zeiss4Me), Shutterstock
(Africa Studio, area381, Dzinnik Darius, Richard Griffin, Brent
Hofacker, Vitaly Korovin, Neamov, NEGOVURA, Ildi Papp,
photosync, pogonici, prapass, Joshua Resnick, stephen rudolph,
Ekaterina Smirnova, Evlakhov Valeriy, VolkOFF-ZS-BP, Yganko),
SuperStock (The Art Archive, Yagi Studio)

Library of Congress Cataloging-in-Publication Data
Gilbert, Sara. • Chinese food / by Sara Gilbert. • p. cm. —
(Cooking school) • *Summary*: An elementary introduction to the
relationship between cooking and Chinese culture, the effect of
local agriculture on the diets of different regions, common tools
such as woks, and recipe instructions.
Includes bibliographical references
and index. • ISBN 978-1-60818-
501-6 (*hardcover*) • ISBN
978-1-62832-095-4 (*pbk*)
1. Cooking, Chinese—
Juvenile literature. 2. Food—
China—Juvenile literature. I. Title.
TX724.5.C5G48 2015
641.5951—dc23   2014002296

CCSS: RI.1.1, 2, 3, 5, 6, 7; RI.2.1,
2, 3, 5, 6, 7; RI.3.1, 3, 5, 7;
RF.1.1; RF.2.3, 4; RF.3.3

First Edition
9 8 7 6 5 4 3 2 1

Table of Contents

Delicious Foods   4

Skilled Cooks   6

Taste of China   8

Working with Woks   16

You Can Cook!   19

Glossary   24

Read More   24

Websites   24

Index   24

Delicious Foods

People cook everywhere. They cook to feed their families. They cook because it's fun to make delicious, *nutritious* food. Cooking has been an important part of the Chinese *culture* for hundreds of years.

Chow mein is a Chinese dish that means "fried noodles."

Skilled Cooks

Long ago, Chinese rulers called emperors wanted the best cooks to make their meals. Cooks in China try different *ingredients* and *recipes*, but they often cook with rice.

People in China have enjoyed eating together for hundreds of years.

Taste of China

People near the South China Sea like to eat many kinds of meat. They mix meat with vegetables in stir-fries.

Meat and vegetables mix well with lots of noodles, too.

Spicy foods are popular in southwestern China. Cooks use garlic and chili peppers in many meals.

Chili peppers and garlic add spice and flavor to stir-fries.

Near the long Yangtze (*YANG-see*) River, people like to eat fresh fish. They cook with a lot of soy sauce there, too.

Fish caught in the river or the sea can end up on plates in China.

Wheat grows in the northern parts of China. People there eat noodles and pancakes that are filled with meats, fruits, or vegetables.

Chopsticks can hold everything from duck pancakes to wheat noodles.

Working with Woks

Chinese cooks often use heavy iron pans called woks. Woks have round bottoms. They are good for making everything from stir-fries to soup.

Eggrolls

are often served as an *appetizer*.

INGREDIENTS

2 tablespoons oil

1 tablespoon chopped garlic

¼ cup diced onion

½ pound ground pork

5 cups shredded cabbage

egg roll wrappers

salt and pepper

sweet and sour sauce and hot mustard for serving

DIRECTIONS

1. With an adult's help, heat 2 tablespoons oil in a frying pan.

2. Add 1 tablespoon chopped garlic and ¼ cup diced onion to the pan. Then add ½ pound ground pork or other ground meat.

3. When the meat is cooked, add up to 5 cups shredded cabbage and cook 5 minutes. Then add salt and pepper.

4. Spoon 2 tablespoons of the filling in the corner of an egg roll wrapper. Fold over the left side, then the right. Then roll it toward the other corner and press to seal.

5. With an adult's help, fry the roll in hot oil until golden brown. Then eat with sweet and sour sauce or hot mustard.

Fried rice

uses leftover rice, vegetables, and other ingredients.

INGREDIENTS

2 tablespoons oil

chopped peppers, snow peas, and carrots

2 cups cooked rice

2 tablespoons soy sauce

DIRECTIONS

1. With an adult's help, heat 2 tablespoons oil in a frying pan or wok.

2. When the oil is hot, add chopped vegetables such as peppers, snow peas, and carrots, and stir as they cook. You can add meat, garlic, or spices, too.

3. Add up to 2 cups cooked rice and stir occasionally for about 5 minutes. Then add 2 tablespoons soy sauce and cook for another 2 minutes.

4. Enjoy your fried rice warm right away, or eat it cold later!

A stir-fry

is tossed in hot oil.

INGREDIENTS

1 tablespoon oil

cut strips of chicken, beef, or pork

fresh or frozen mixed vegetables

2 tablespoons soy sauce

rice for serving

DIRECTIONS

1. With an adult's help, heat 1 tablespoon oil in a frying pan or wok.

2. Add strips of chicken, beef, or pork, and cook thoroughly.

3. Add fresh or frozen cut vegetables and 2 tablespoons soy sauce. Cook for a couple minutes.

4. When it is hot, serve your stir-fry over rice.

Glossary

appetizer a small serving of food eaten before the main meal

culture the artistic and social traditions of a group of people

ingredients any of the foods or liquids that combine to complete a recipe

nutritious healthy and good for you

recipes sets of instructions for making a certain dish, including a list of ingredients

Read More

Blaxland, Wendy. *I Can Cook! Chinese Food*. Mankato, Minn.: Smart Apple Media, 2011.

Low, Jennifer. *Kitchen for Kids*. New York: Whitecap Books, 2010.

Simonds, Nina. *Moonbeams, Dumplings & Dragon Boats: A Treasury of Chinese Holiday Tales, Activities & Recipes*. Boston: Houghton Mifflin Harcourt, 2002.

Websites

http://www.pbs.org/food/theme/cooking-with-kids/
Find easy recipes to try by yourself or with an adult's assistance.

http://www.foodnetwork.com/cooking-with-kids/package/index.html
Learn to cook with celebrity chefs on the website of television's Food Network.

Note: Every effort has been made to ensure that the websites listed above are suitable for children, that they have educational value, and that they contain no inappropriate material. However, because of the nature of the Internet, it is impossible to guarantee that these sites will remain active indefinitely or that their contents will not be altered.

Index

chili peppers *11*

cooking *4, 6, 13*

egg rolls *19*

emperors *6*

garlic *11, 19, 21*

meats *8, 13, 15, 19, 21, 23*

noodles *15*

pancakes *15*

recipes *6, 19, 21, 23*

rice *6, 21, 23*

South China Sea *8*

soy sauce *13, 21, 23*

stir-fries *8, 16, 23*

vegetables *8, 15, 19, 21, 23*

woks *16, 21, 23*

Yangtze River *13*